PRESENTED TO

_____

FROM  W9-BEP-412

_____

DATE

_____

December 31

Go call someone right now. Lift them up in ways they can't lift themselves. Send them a text message and say you're sorry. I know they don't deserve it. You didn't either. Don't put a toe in the water with your love; grab your knees and do a cannonball. Move from the bleachers to the field, and you won't ever be the same.

Heaven is watching us,
knowing full well
all that will be left standing in the end
is our love.

We're all learning about loving our
enemies. Draw a circle around yourself,
and go love the people in that circle.
Fill it with difficult people,
the ones you've been avoiding,
the ones you disagree with,
and the ones who are
hard to get along with.

You can no longer continue to be the person you've been. What are you going to let go of? Who is it you don't get? Who don't you understand? Who have you been playing it safe with, while politely keeping your distance? Who has been mean or rude or flat wrong or creeps you out? Don't tell them all your opinions; give them all your love.

January 2

It's better to spend more time loving people than just agreeing with Jesus that people ought to be loved.

There is no love without justice,
but there is no justice without love.

To follow Jesus' example, instead of telling people what Jesus means, we can just love people the way He did.

Loving our enemies
has always been God's idea, not ours.
The people who creep us out
aren't obstacles to having faith;
they're opportunities to understanding it.

It's hard to believe Jesus loves thieves and all the difficult people we've met just the same as you and me. Yet the incredible message Love came to Earth to give was that we're all tied for first in God's mind.

Loving people the way Jesus did
means being constantly misunderstood.
People who are becoming love don't care.
They will do whatever it takes
to reach whoever is hurting.

God doesn't want us to just study Him
like He's an academic project.
He wants us to become love.

Loving your enemies
doesn't just mean learning about them
or being nice to them or tolerating them.
It means helping them.

We're all rough drafts
of the people we're still becoming.

Jesus said being right with Him
meant loving people
who go at things wrong.

We don't need to be who we used to be;
God sees who we're becoming—
and we're becoming love.

December 23

Even the evilest of people
have nothing compared to
the kind of power love has.

Jesus talked to His friends a lot about how we should identify ourselves. He said it wouldn't be what we said we believed or all the good we hoped to do someday. Nope, He said we would identify ourselves simply by how we loved people.

Love always
multiplies itself.

Love isn't something we fall into;
love is someone we become.

Don't talk to the people you love about their failures and the dark places they've been. Talk to them about who they're becoming and the bright hope that is their future. Speak truthful and wise words over them. Pin medals on their chest, look them in the eye, and tell them, "Look how far you've come."

It's easy to love kind, lovely, humble people. Who wouldn't? It's much easier to avoid the people we don't understand and the ones who live differently than us than to love them. But love is our goal.

People who are becoming love celebrate how far the people around them have come. They're constantly asking the question, "Where do you want to go?" Then they help the people around them get there.

Are we spending our whole lives avoiding the type of people Jesus spent His whole life engaging?

It's easy to confuse busyness with progress
and accomplishments with pleasing Jesus.
Every day we get to decide whether
we're really following Jesus
or treating Him like He's just a Sherpa
carrying our stuff.

God's idea isn't that we would just give
and receive love but that we
could actually become love.

It's hard to walk with Jesus
and run ahead of Him at the same time.

People who are becoming love see the beauty in others even when their off-putting behavior makes for a pretty weird mask. What Jesus told His friends can be summed up in this way: He wants us to love everybody—always—and start with the people who creep us out.

Faith isn't a business trip
walked on a sidewalk;
it's an adventure
worked out on a steep
and sometimes difficult trail.

God gave us discernment, and we should use it as we live our lives. He's also given us love and understanding and kindness and the ability to forgive, which have power we often leave untapped.

December 16

We're all going to trip as we try to follow Him through the difficult terrain of our lives. But when we do, we'll bump into Him all over again. Following Jesus means climbing, tripping, dusting ourselves off, and climbing some more.

January 15

There's a difference between having good judgment and living in judgment. The trick is to use lots of the first and to go a little lighter on the second.

Here's what I've learned:
When you've got a guide you can trust,
you don't have to worry about the path
you're on. It's the same lesson I've been
learning about Jesus. I'm just trying
to follow love's lead.

The thing about love is that we have to tackle a good amount of fear to love people who are difficult.

December 14

It's hard to ignore that most of the people
doing the talking from up front are guys
like me who seem pretty nice and are
relatable. They make us feel comfortable.
Yet the people Jesus used more often were
the ones who had messed up big
and were desperate.

Jesus showed us what it means to become
love when He spent His last meal with a
man He knew would betray Him and then
willingly died a criminal's death.

Jesus chose fishermen who rarely
got their nets on the right side of the boat.
By all accounts, even after they had been
with Jesus for three years, they still
didn't fully understand Who He was.
They were imperfect, were flawed,
and had failed—sometimes big.
Grace never seems fair
until you need some.

We make loving people a lot more
complicated than Jesus did.

December 12

Jesus said He would turn us into love
if we were willing to leave behind
who we used to be.

Am I really so insecure that I surround myself only with people who agree with me? When people are flat wrong, why do I appoint myself the sheriff to straighten them out? Burning down others' opinions doesn't make us right. It makes us arsonists.

Maybe God made loving Him
and our enemies the easiest way to tell
whether we just agree with Jesus or if we
want to be perfect like Him.

God's endgame has always been the same.
He wants our hearts to be His.

Jesus explained the reason He wanted us to love our enemies was so we could be perfect, the way His Father in Heaven is perfect. Our problem following Jesus is, we're trying to be a better version of us rather than a more accurate reflection of Him.

God wants us to love the people near us
and love the people we've kept far away.
To do this, He wants us
to live without fear.

December 9

Paul was one of the people who talked about Jesus. He explained grace in this way: He said neither death nor life, neither angels nor demons, neither present nor future, nor any powers, neither height nor depth, nor anything else in all creation could ever separate us from the love of God.

God wants us to grow love in our hearts
and then cultivate it by the acre
in the world.

On the day Jesus died on the cross, He was broken for us. It was like God was saying, "What's been done today will never be undone."

January 23

We'll become in our lives
what we do with our love.

Jesus didn't come to make us look like
we've got it together. He came to let us
know how to be like Him.

Those who are becoming love
don't throw people off roofs;
they lower people through them instead.

December 6

Jesus was talking to His friends one day and explained how He wanted us to live our lives. He pulled His friends in close and said something I bet surprised them. He didn't say they needed to use bigger words in their prayers, or go to church more, or not chew tobacco or dance. It wasn't behaviors He talked about. He said if we wanted to please God, we needed to love our enemies.

If we really want to "meet Jesus,"
then we have to get a lot closer
to the people He created.
All of them, not just some of them.

December 5

What is it you don't think you can do?
What do you think is too big for you, or
too scary, or too risky? Sometimes God
whispers it, and sometimes He shouts it.
Whatever the volume, I bet He's always
using the same three words with us:
Be. Not. Afraid.

I think Jesus' plan all along has been for us
to meet the people He made
and feel like we just met Him.

I have a red plate at home that says I am "very special." We get it out on birthdays. The plate doesn't make me special though. It's the people surrounding me and my plate who make me special.
The same is true for you.

Certainly God wants us to learn about Him by reading the letters and stories collected in the Bible, but He also wants us to meet Him by loving the people who are difficult to get along with.

December 3

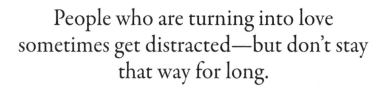

People who are turning into love
sometimes get distracted—but don't stay
that way for long.

If I'm only willing to love the people who
are nice to me, the ones who see things
the way I do, and avoid all the rest, it's like
reading every other page of the Bible
and thinking I know what it says.

December 2

Great love
often involves tremendous risk.

Jesus told His friends if they wanted to be like Him, they needed to love their neighbors and they needed to love difficult people.

Sometimes we wait for permission or a plan or a calling or a mystical sign from God before we get started. It could work that way I suppose. What I've found, though, is when we're looking for a plan, God often sends us a person.

Not once did Jesus gather His friends around Him and say, "Guys, I just want you to agree with Me." He wants us to do what He said, and He said He wants us to love everybody always.

God said He picked us, and that's all I
need to know to be part of the celebration.
We're the bride of Christ, not because of
what we look like but because
of Who we are trying to act like.

Jesus said to love our enemies.
He meant we should love the people we
don't understand. The ones we disagree
with. The ones who are flat wrong about
more than a couple of things.
We all have plenty of those people in our
lives. In fact, we are probably one
of those people sometimes.

To God, we look just terrific.
Does our church have problems?
You bet.
But He continues to pick us
to spread His love to the world.

God allows all of us to go missing a time or two. When we do, He doesn't pout or withhold His love the way we probably would if someone completely ignored us or walked away from us. Instead, He pursues us in love.

Perhaps if we spent a little more time
looking at Jesus,
we'd start seeing ourselves
the way He does.

God doesn't try to find us;
He always knows where we are.
Rather, He goes with us
as we find ourselves.

God doesn't hold up a scorecard as we walk by. He sees Jesus. It's that simple. The way our church will return to the loving and accepting place the Bible talks about is by keeping our eyes on the Groom instead of one another. We can put all the scorecards away.

We have both a little sheep
and some shepherd in us too.
God isn't constantly telling us
what to do as we search for ourselves.
He gently reminds us who we are.

God loves us, and He wants
to spend forever together.
We're His bride.
He doesn't see all our flaws;
He just sees us.

God continues to rewrite our lives in
beautiful and unexpected ways, knowing
the next version of us will usually be
better than the previous one.

Do you know what makes a bride look terrific?
It's not the fancy dress or the building or the
flowers or the music. Those things are great, but
what makes the bride look terrific is everyone in
the room knows the groom chose her to be his
and she's chosen him to be hers.
The two of them can't wait to spend forever
together. I think this is the reason why
God calls us His bride.

It's possible to be correct and not right. We do this most often when we have the right words and the wrong heart. Sadly, whenever we make our opinions more important than the difficult people God made, we turn the wine back into water.

Every time we go to church and point fingers at each other, we betray Jesus with another kiss. At "our" church, we go there to meet Him, not to critique each other.

Arguments won't change people.
Simply giving away kindness won't either.
Only Jesus has the power to change
people, and it will be harder for them
to see Jesus if their view of Him
is blocked by our big opinions.

Seriously, walk up behind someone who is hurting and lift them right off the ground. Don't be creepy about it, but do it. You won't need to tell them you're praying for them—they'll know. If you're wondering where Jesus' friends are, just find people whose feet are a foot off the ground because someone else is lifting them up. You just found our church.

February 7

I used to think we'd be known for whom
we hung around, the groups or social
issues we identified with, or the faith
tradition we were familiar with.
Now I think while we might be known
for our opinions, we'll be remembered
for our love.

We don't need to just talk about lifting others up in prayer when they're hurting. Actually lift one another up instead.

We only really find our identities by engaging the people we've been avoiding.

Even if you don't think you go to a church, you're part of our church. At our church, there is nothing to join, just Jesus. This is probably why Jesus told His friends, where two or more people who follow Him go, He's there.

Jesus gave us three simple and seemingly
impossible ideas for us to follow:
love Him, love your neighbor,
and love your enemies.

Should we meet together
as a community around Jesus?
Yes, constantly. Where? Everywhere.
You pick. He wants our hearts;
He doesn't care about the address
where it happens.

February 10

Jesus came to Earth and declared He would turn God's enemies into His friends. He didn't do it with twenty-dollar words or lectures or by waving a bony finger at people who had made mistakes. He convinces us with love, and He does it without fear or shame.

Does God use church buildings?
You bet. Does He love it when we gather
for worship in them? Absolutely. Nothing
delights Him more. Does He need them?
Not for a minute. He's got us, we've got
Him, and He's given us each other.

Jesus doesn't raise His voice and shout
over the noise in our lives.
He lets the power of love
do all the talking for Him.
We have the same shot
in other people's lives every day.

Perhaps we thought because God made us, we should make something nice for Him in return, so we built Him a bunch of buildings and started going to them on Sunday mornings and Wednesday nights. I love church buildings. I spend almost every weekend in one. The problem is, God said He doesn't dwell in buildings made by men; instead, we can find Him in the people He made who want their lives to look like His.

Loving each other is what we were meant to do and how we were made to roll.

Church is made of people like you and me whom Jesus didn't pass over just because we messed up. He didn't give us a membership; He gave us a message.

Loving each other
is not where we start when we begin
following Jesus; it's the beautiful path
we travel the rest of our lives.

Jesus wanted us to live into the beautiful, unique creations God made us to be. Simply put, we can be "one" without being each other.

February 14

Will loving others the way Jesus said to love them be messy and ambiguous and uncomfortable? You bet it will.
Will we be misunderstood? Constantly.
But extravagant love often means coloring outside the lines and going beyond the norm.

Jesus prayed for unity, not sameness.
He knew the gospel wasn't a bunch of
rules to obey; it was a Person
to follow and be one with.

Loving the neighbors we don't understand takes work and humility and patience and guts. It means leaving the security of our easy relationships to engage in some tremendously awkward ones.

The night before Jesus died,
His prayer for us
was that we would be "one."
He knew what it was like to be "one"
with His Father, and He said
He wanted that for us.

Find a way to love difficult people more, and you'll be living the life Jesus talked about. Go find someone you've been avoiding, and give away extravagant love to them.

People who are becoming love
lose all the labels
because they know
they don't need them.

Love the hard ones,
and you'll learn more about God,
your neighbor,
your enemies,
and your faith.

Jesus is more interested
in making us grow
than having us look finished.
He wants us to realize
we're just not quite there yet.

February 18

Find someone you think is wrong, someone you disagree with, someone who isn't like you at all, and decide to love that person the way you want Jesus to love you.

Instead of wishing you were the person who had it all figured out, listen for the gentle and kind voice of Jesus reminding you to stop laying sod where He's planting seed in your life.

We need to love everybody always.
Jesus never said doing these things
would be easy. He just said it would work.

Jesus never had a problem with people who knew their shortcomings; He didn't tolerate people who faked it. Once we get real with where we actually are and our desperate need for Him, He's got a person He can do something with.

God doesn't just give us promises;
He gives us each other.

Even in our imperfections,
God is over the moon about us anyway,
and He'll help us find the strength
and courage to change.

When some of Jesus' friends were arguing about who would get to sit closer to Him when they got to Heaven, Jesus told them unless they changed and became like children, they'd never enter the Kingdom of God. I think what He was saying is, we need a childlike faith to understand Him.

God doesn't measure things
the way we do,
and He doesn't grade us
on a curve.

It's not acting childish that will get us to Heaven. Plenty of people do that. It won't be our big prayers and fancy language that will help us get there either. Big faith doesn't need big words. We also don't need to make faith easier, because it's not; we need to make it simpler, because it is.

Jesus is the only one who ever loved people perfectly. None of us will ever get love and kindness or sacrifice entirely right. We're all just doing the best we can.

One of the things about kids, in addition
to their simple faith, is they aren't afraid of
the things many of us are afraid of.
Their curiosity about what they don't
know outdistances their fears
about what they do know by a mile.

It's this simple and that difficult: The guy who is up in front at church needs to be the same guy in the back of the rental car line. If you can't do that, either stop driving or get off the stage.

Three words stand out to me in the Bible.
They aren't big and deep and theological
words, yet that's probably what makes
them big and deep and theological in
nature. Here they are: Be. Not. Afraid.

Knowing things about the Bible is terrific. But I'd trade in a dozen Bible studies for a bucket full of acceptance—and truth be told, so would everyone around us.

Be. Not. Afraid.
These words have exactly as much power
as we give them in our lives.

People don't grow where they're planted;
they grow where they're loved.

People who are becoming love experience
the same uncertainties we all do.
They just stop letting fear call the shots.

November 3

We all encounter difficulties.
It's what we do next that defines us.

If we take to heart Jesus' words about having a childlike faith and not being afraid, they can move us from merely wishing things would get better for us to bearing up under the circumstances God actually gives us.

November 2

As much as I'd like to make it more complicated and have more steps so I can find some cover for my inaction, it's really simple. Loving my neighbors means I have to find a new way to engage them. To pull this off, I need to do it with an unreasonable amount of patience and kindness and understanding.

Having a childlike faith and not being
afraid lets us move from running away and
hiding from our problems to engaging
and embracing them.

It's taken some time, but I'm starting to act like my purpose is to love God and to love the people around me the way Jesus loved the people around Him.

Having a childlike faith and not being afraid can fill us with quiet confidence and contagious hope.

We can pretend to have all the game we want to up on stage, in the pulpit, on the field, at work, or in our faith communities. But it's how we engage with the rental car attendant or the grocery bagger or the bank teller or the person who puts on the car tires that lets everybody know where we really are with Jesus.

What's crazy is, when we're not afraid and engage the world with a childlike faith, the people around us won't be afraid either.

One thing I've learned from Jesus is, extravagant love is never wasted. Yours won't be either if you keep running home.

March 2

When we let them,
hope and courage will spread like a cold.
A really good kind of cold.

We will become in our lives what we put in our buckets. If we fill our buckets with a bunch of business deals, we'll turn into businesspeople. If we fill them with arguments, we'll become lawyers. If we fill them with a critical spirit, we'll become cynics. If we fill them with joy, we'll experience tremendous happiness.

"Love one another." What is simple often isn't easy; what is easy often doesn't last.

If our lives aren't working for the people around us, our lives aren't working for us.

Sometimes we are looking for a plan, but Jesus tells us about our purpose instead: He says it is to love God with all our heart and soul and mind.

How is your life working
for the people around you?

Sometimes we see loving God
and loving our neighbors
as two separate ideas,
but Jesus saw them
as one inseparable mandate.

When we get to Heaven,
Jesus said, He will want to know how we
treated the ones who have failed the worst.

Jesus knows we can't love God if we don't love the people He surrounds us with.

Jesus lets us participate in helping those in
need, if we're willing, so we'll learn more
about how He feels about us and
how He feels about the people
we may have been avoiding.

March 7

We can stop waiting for a plan
and just go love everybody.
There's no school to learn how to love your
neighbor, just the house next door.

October 24

Jesus doesn't need our help with the hungry or thirsty or sick or strange or naked or people in jails. I know this because I asked Him. He wants our hearts.

No one expects us to love our neighbor
flawlessly, but we can love them fearlessly,
furiously, and unreasonably.

I once heard someone say,
"If you want applause, join the circus."
If you want to talk about it with Jesus
forever, keep it quiet.

We're not supposed to love only our neighbors, but Jesus thought we should start with them. He knew if our love isn't going to work for the people who live close to us, then it's probably not going to work for the rest of the world.

When you do something for Jesus while He appears to be hungry or sick or thirsty or strange or naked or in jail, don't mess it up by making a big deal out of it.

Jesus wasn't specific
about who our neighbors are,
probably so we wouldn't start making lists
of those we don't need to love.

October 21

Jesus knew some of us would be tempted to tell everyone who would listen about all the things we'd done. He said if we made a big deal about what we'd done now, hoping to get someone to clap, we would have had our reward. We don't need to be the hero in everyone's story. Jesus already landed that part.

Each of us is surrounded every day by our neighbors. They're ahead of us, behind us, on each side of us. They're every place we go. It's one thing we all have in common: We're all somebody's neighbor, and they're ours.

If we make everything about us,
it'll never be about Jesus.

This has been God's simple yet brilliant
master plan from the beginning:
He made a whole world of neighbors.
We call it Earth, but God just calls it
a really big neighborhood.

When we do things for the poor
or the sick or the strange or the naked
or those in jail, Jesus already knows
all about it because it's Him.

What often keeps us from loving our neighbors is fear of what will happen if we do. Frankly, what scares me more is thinking about what will happen if we don't.

We don't need to keep track of all the good things we do for God. In fact, He said to do just the opposite. Jesus talked about not letting one of your hands even know what the other is up to.

Being fearless isn't something
we can decide to be in a moment,
but fear can be overcome
with time and the right help.

I don't want what's "fair" anymore.
I want to be like Jesus.
It's a distinction worth making.

We can bring all the game we've got,
but only Jesus has the power to call out
of us the kind of courage it takes to live
the life He talked about.

Do selfless things and you'll not only find
your faith again; you'll find Jesus.
Even better, you'll have plenty of things
to talk to Him about for eternity in
Heaven. That's the plan.

We can't love people we don't know.
Saying we love our neighbors is simple.
But guess what? Doing it is too.

Don't make it more complicated than it is.
Just start. Go find someone who is hungry
right now, and do something about it.
I've heard lots of people say that giving
the poor a fishing pole is better than giving
them a meal, but I don't see them giving
away many fish or poles.

Jesus' command to "love your neighbor" isn't a metaphor for something else. We think it means we're supposed to actually love our neighbors.

Jesus said His plan for all of us was to love Him and then find people who are hungry or thirsty or who feel like strangers or are sick or don't have clothes or are in prison or creep us out or are our enemies and go love them just like they were Him.

Engage them.
Delight in them.
Throw a party for them.
When joy is a habit,
love is a reflex.

Jesus said if we wanted to do something nice for God, we'd do it for His kids. And we don't need to make a big deal out of it either. He'll find out. Good fathers do.

God didn't give us neighbors
to be our projects;
He surrounded us with them
to be our teachers.

Jesus said when we give away love freely to one another and meet the needs of poor and needy and isolated and hurting people, we're actually doing it for Him.

Selfless love has the power to transform
even the darkest places into meadows.

People who are becoming love think every needy person they meet is Jesus. And they make it look easy to have all the time in the world for others.

Besides the streets of Heaven
being paved in gold, I'm also kind of
hoping they're lined with balloons.

At the end of our lives, God will care most about how we treated the people on the fringes of our lives. He'll want to talk about whether we gave them a hug or some much needed help. All of this because He said if we did kind things for the lonely and hurting and isolated in the world, we were really doing it for Him.

When we get to Heaven,
I bet we'll find Jesus blowing us kisses,
rubbing our noses, and welcoming us to
our next neighborhood.

What big idea do you have that you've not pursued because you didn't know if it would work? Who have you wanted to reach out to in love but were afraid you'd be rejected? Who has broken your heart? Who misunderstood you? Who do you need to forgive? Now's your time. Don't wait any longer. You know what to do. You've got this. You know enough.

March 23

Instead of telling people what they want,
we need to tell them who they are.
This works every time.

Sometimes God is confidently quiet.
He doesn't give us more explanations.
He knows we don't need more words of
instruction. The moment we take even a
tiny shuffle forward, what God is already
thinking about us is this: I love you.
You've got this. You know enough.

We'll become in our lives whoever the
people we love the most say we are.

God didn't promise us a safe life. Instead, He said He would give us a dangerous, courageous, and purposeful one if we'll take Him at His word and stay engaged.

God told Moses he was a leader, and Moses became one. He told Peter he was a rock, and he led the church. If we want to love people the way God loved people, let God's Spirit do the talking when it comes to telling people what they want.

God knows that without risk,
we can't grow.

All the directions we're giving to each other aren't getting people to the feet of Jesus. More often, the unintended result is they lead these people back to us.

I picture God sitting beside each of us, not confused or afraid but confident we have all the information we need. We may not have had experience with the circumstances we're presently facing, but He's allowed us to experience a lifetime of other things to prepare us for what is coming next.

When we make ourselves the hall
monitors of other people's behavior,
we risk having approval become more
important than Jesus' love.

October 4

God is with us, and He's not ever entirely silent. He's sent us books about Him and has included a lot of letters, and He's sent us friends too. He's given us successes and failures—plenty of both. He's written things on our hearts like love and grace and patience and compassion so we can write those things on the hearts of our friends. We're God's calligraphy.

Faith lasts a lifetime and will carry us
through the most difficult of times
without a word being spoken.

If we're fortunate, God surrounds us
with friends who know us so well they've
stopped trying to control our conduct
with endless instructions and instead trust
that God is at work in our lives, even if
He's doing things we don't yet understand.

Telling people what they should want
turns us into a bunch of sheriffs.
People who are becoming love
lose the badge
and give away grace instead.

Most of us don't need more instructions;
we simply need someone
who believes in us.

Tell the people you meet who they're becoming, and trust that God will help people find their way toward beautiful things in their lives without you.

God already believes in you. He's so confident we already know what to do next that He's willing to be silent even when we ask for His voice. He doesn't care as much as we do whether we perform perfectly or not. He just wants us to be His while we do it.

You've probably messed up a couple of times. Me too. Run back toward God, not away from Him.

There's a verse in the Bible that says,
"Do not despise these small beginnings."
I love that. It's a reminder to me that God
doesn't just value the big endeavors that
work and He isn't afraid we'll fail;
instead, He delights in our attempts.

Do lots of finding your way back to the people you've loved and who have loved you. Figure out who you've broken your rhythm with. Don't let the misunderstanding decide your future.

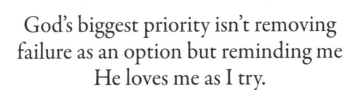

God's biggest priority isn't removing failure as an option but reminding me He loves me as I try.

If you've lost your way with God,
let Him close the distance between you
and start the celebration again.

God knows what He's taught me.
He's seen when I've succeeded and when
I've failed. From His point of view, that all
rolls up into an unspoken whisper from
Him I can almost hear saying,
"You've got this."

April 3

We're all in the same truck
when it comes to our need for love and
acceptance and forgiveness.

There have been times when I wanted to hear God's voice—particularly when something really big mattered to me. The sad truth is, I'm often making too much racket to hear Him. He won't try to shout over all the noise in our lives to get our attention. He speaks most clearly in the stillness desperation brings.

Jesus doesn't give us a bunch of directions intended to manipulate our behavior or control our conduct. Instead, He has beautiful hopes for us and has told us what those are, but He isn't scowling at us when we're not yet ready to have those same hopes for ourselves.

What a shame it would be if we were waiting for God to say something while He's been waiting on us to do something. He speaks to me the loudest on the way. Simply put, if we want more faith, we need to do more stuff.

April 5

Jesus won't love us more or less based on how we act, and He's more interested in our hearts than all the things we do.

The people who have shaped my faith the most didn't try to teach me anything; they let me know they trusted me. And that taught me everything.

Jesus isn't stuck telling us what to do,
when to do it, or what we want.
Far better, He continues to tell us through
our successes and our mistakes who we are,
and here's what He wants us to know—
we are His.

God isn't always leading us to the safest route forward but to the one where we'll grow the most.

April 7

Don't build a castle
when you can build a kingdom.

God doesn't give us all the details, because
He trusts us.

We need every type of prayer, I suppose, but I don't think we need to sound like each other. God isn't wowed by fancy words; He delights in humble hearts.

Great love expressing itself in the world doesn't need any arm waving; it's always recognizable and leaves little doubt in the lives of the people it touches.

Jesus told His friends we weren't supposed
to spend our lives building castles.
He said He wanted us to build a kingdom,
and there's a big difference between
building a castle and building a kingdom.

People who are becoming love don't think about what they've lost. They think about what they'll do with what they still have. And the answer is much.

Castles have moats
to keep creepy people out,
but kingdoms have bridges
to let everyone in.

People who are becoming love aren't stuck trying to figure out why things happen to them; they're too busy celebrating other people's lives and making things happen for them.

Castles have dungeons
for people who have messed up,
but kingdoms have grace.

People who are becoming love see power
in their brokenness and opportunities in
the opposition they face.

Castles have trolls.
You've probably met a couple.
Trolls aren't bad people; they're just hard
to understand. Here's the deal: It's how we
treat the trolls in our lives that will let us
know how far along we are in our faith.

People who have developed a friendship with Jesus and are becoming love aren't immune to life's setbacks. They have just as many as everyone else. But they know they're neither defined nor limited by their circumstances.

April 13

If we want a kingdom, then we start the way grace did, by drawing a circle around everyone and saying they're in.

September 17

When we're busy getting our validation from the people around us, we stop looking for it from God.

Kingdoms are built
from the people up.
There's no set of plans—just Jesus.

We need to be careful where our minds dwell. Many of us dwell on what other people are thinking of us. It's easy to do. But we can be so busy trying to get the approval of others that we forget who Jesus said we are.

The people I see as problems, God sees as
sons and daughters made in His image.
The people I see as difficult,
He sees as delightfully different.

September 15

It doesn't matter whether it's
comparison or distraction or escape
that turns our heads—what we look
at will be the difference
between a great dive
and a big disaster.

The fact is, what skews my view of people who are sometimes hard to be around is that God is working on different things in their lives than He is working on in mine.

September 14

Where we turn our heads
is where we'll land with our lives.

God knows we're easily confused
and often wayward,
and He pursues us with love anyway.

Jesus tells us to bring what we have to Him, and He will make something amazing out of it.

God wants us to see things
the way He does, and it's not going to
happen from the top floor of our castles.
It will happen at the ground level of grace.

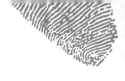

We're not held back
by what we don't have
but by what we don't use.

God wants me to love the ones I don't
understand, to get to know their names.
To invite them to do things with me.
To go and find the ones everyone has
shunned and turned away. To see them as
my neighbors even if we are
in totally different places.

I used to think it would take a lifetime to become someone's friend, but now I think we do it just three minutes at a time. It's the way Jesus made friends with most of the people He met, and it's a great way for us to engage the people around us, including the ones we've been avoiding.

You'll be able to spot people who are becoming love because they want to build kingdoms, not castles. They fill their lives with people who don't look like them or act like them or even believe the same things as them. They treat them with love and respect and are more eager to learn from them than presume they have something to teach.

God never promised
we'd have all the answers.
What He offers to us is a box of crayons
and the opportunity to let love draw
bigger circles around the people we meet
than they thought were possible.

What part are you going to play in
building the kind of kingdom Jesus said
would outlast us all?

September 9

People who are becoming love
don't swing at every pitch.
We start by meeting people
just three minutes at a time.
Don't waste a minute of it arguing with
people who are wrong. Quietly delight in
the confidence that comes from having
found truth in your own life.

The word "with" is much bigger and
worthier and more accessible than any ten
Bible verses. It's God's purpose for us.
It's the reason Jesus came. It's the whole
Bible in a word. People who are becoming
love are "with" those who are hurting
and help them get home.

September 8

When we understand ourselves
from the perspective of God's love,
we start to see that our time here isn't
meant to be spent forming opinions about
the people we meet. It's an opportunity
to draw the kind of circles around them
that grace has drawn around us, until
everybody is on the inside.

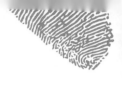

I've always thought that people
who didn't want to be with people here
are going to hate Heaven.
Heaven will be all about people.

When we draw a circle
around the whole world like grace did
and say everybody is in, God's love
gives us bigger identities
than we used to have.

Jesus told His friends that letting people
see the way we love each other
would be the best way
to let people know about Him.

September 6

Jesus championed a backward economy.
He said if people wanted to be at the front
of the line, they needed to go to the back.
If they wanted to be a good leader,
they would need to be an even better follower.
If they wanted to know Him better,
they'd need to stop thinking so much about
themselves, and if they wanted to love Him
more, they needed to love each other more.

The best way to let people know about Jesus isn't giving them a lot of directions or instructions or having them memorize or study all the right things. It will happen when someone meets you or me and feels as if they've just met Jesus.

He said we can each get a new identity
in Him. The people who take Him up
on this offer begin to define success and
failure the way He did. They move from
merely identifying with someone's pain to
standing with them in it and from having a
bunch of opinions to giving away love
and grace freely.

Jesus wants someone who meets
a person who loves Him to feel
like they have just met heaven.

The beautiful message of Jesus is His invitation to everyone that they can trade in who they used to be for who God sees them becoming.

This is our job; it's always been our job:
We're supposed to just love
the people in front of us. We're the ones
who tell them who they are.

When Jesus invaded history, it was as if He stood at the front of a long line of people—everyone who has ever lived or will live. He asked all of us if we knew who we were, and He asked us who we thought He was. Some got it right and some didn't. The same is still true today.

We don't need to spend as much time as we do telling people what we think about what they're doing. Loving people doesn't mean we need to control their conduct. There's a big difference between the two. Loving people means caring without an agenda.

If at this point you've only heard of Jesus,
ask Him who He is.
I bet He'll let you know.

As soon as we have an agenda,
it's not love anymore. It's acting like you
care to get someone to do what you want
or what you think God wants them to do.
Do less of that, and people will see
a lot less of you and more of Jesus.

If you're already friends with Jesus, don't get in everyone else's way as they figure it out with Him. Just love them and point them in His direction.

April 30

Talk behind each other's backs constantly.
Just talk about the right stuff.
Talk about Jesus.
Talk about grace.
Talk about love and acceptance.

We can tell the people we meet about Jesus. When I've tried and it worked, what I often found is I'd led people to me, not Him. If we take Jesus at His word, people won't know who Jesus is because we've told them; they'll know because Jesus let them know.

People don't grow
where they are informed; they grow
where they're loved and accepted.

I've sometimes thought
I'd make a lousy evangelist because
I don't think we lead people to Jesus.
I think Jesus leads people to Jesus.

May 2

Talk about who people are becoming and
who you see them turning into.
And give people medals, lots of them.
The people around us should be walking
around looking like the chairman
of the Joint Chiefs of Staff.
They should jingle when they walk.

God wants to use people like us
to show the world what we know about
Jesus by having them see the way
we love the people around us,
particularly the difficult ones.

It's this simple: I want people to meet
you and me and feel like they've just
experienced Heaven.

Jesus wants us to show people
who He is by what we do,
not just tell them what we think.

May 4

God was with us
so we'd be with each other.

When what our faith looks like becomes
more important than what it is, it's
evidence we've forgotten who we really
are. God constantly allows things
to happen in our lives that help us
understand where we are with Him
and who we really are in the context
of our circumstances.

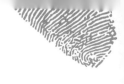

The Christmas story tells us God said,
"The virgin will conceive and give birth to
a Son, and they will call Him 'Immanuel.'"
Immanuel means "God with us."

Friendships can last a lifetime,
but we make them three minutes at a time.

When God sent Jesus into the world, He
demonstrated He didn't just want to be an
observer in the lives of the ones He loved.
He wanted to be a participant. He wanted
to be with the ones He loved.

Keep running your race. Is it going to be easy? Heck no. You might even question a couple of times if it's worth it. Jesus is standing at the edge of eternity calling your name. He wants you to run toward Him as fast as your legs will carry you.

There's a big difference between knowing what someone's doing and being with them while they do it. Jesus wasn't sent because God was mad at us. He jumped out of Heaven and came as Immanuel because He wanted to be God with us.

It's not what you look at;
it's what you see.

What I've been doing with my faith is
this: Instead of saying I'm going to believe
in Jesus for my whole life,
I've been trying to actually
obey Jesus for thirty seconds at a time.

Figure out what Jesus' voice sounds like in your life. He's standing at the end of the track, calling your name.
Run as fast as you can in His direction.

Instead of agreeing with all of the difficult commands of Jesus, try to obey God for thirty seconds at a time.

God doesn't just give us Himself.
Sometimes He gives us a few other people
in our lives whose voices we can trust.

Try to love the person in front of you the way Jesus did for the next thirty seconds rather than merely agreeing with Jesus and avoiding them entirely.

The promise Jesus made to His friends was simply this: He promised to be a voice they could trust. All He asked His friends to do was to run toward it.

Try to see difficult people in front of you
for who they could become someday,
and keep reminding yourself about this
possibility for thirty seconds at a time.

God doesn't like us
more when we succeed
or less when we fail.
He delights in our attempts.

It's easy to agree with what Jesus said. What's hard is actually doing what Jesus did. Agreeing is cheap, and obeying is costly.

We all have a tendency to wander.
Sometimes we know what caused us to
stop running in a straight line, and other
times we don't. We crash and burn and
usually don't know what happened.
It's what happens next that will tell
a lot about who we're becoming.

Obeying is costly because it's uncomfortable. It makes us grow one decision and one discussion at a time. It makes us put away our pride. These are the kinds of decisions that aren't made once for a lifetime; they're made thirty seconds at a time.

People who are becoming love
try impossible things
because they've surrounded themselves
with voices they can trust.

God's plan for our renewal
is that we cut away all the things
hanging us up and start all over again
each day with Him.

Keep your eyes fixed on Jesus.
He sees who we're becoming,
and He wants us to become love.

Jesus talked about cutting away things that entangle us and about pruning. If we get the wrong things over the top of our lives, we might look good for a short time, but we won't land our lives well.

Sometimes when we ask for an answer,
God sends us a companion.
They often come in blue jeans,
but they could also be wearing a
stethoscope and a white doctor's coat.

If we want to be like Jesus,
here's our simple and courageous job:
Catch people on the bounce.
When they mess up,
reach out to them with love
and acceptance the way Jesus did.

August 15

I think some of the miracles God does in our lives happen in stages. Even though we've been touched by God, we still don't see people for who they are until something more happens in us.

When people hit hard,
run to them with your arms wide open to
hug them even harder. God wants to be
with them when they mess up,
and He wants us to participate.

What Jesus is looking for are honest answers about what's really going on in our lives, not a bunch of spin.
The reason is simple.
If we fake it and say we're just fine when we're not, we won't actually be healed.

May 18

Find what the people you love
want to do and then go be with them in it.
If my son wanted to make pizzas,
I'd grow the tomatoes.
Be with each other.

There are quite a few people who may have bumped into Jesus along the way, but it didn't stick the first time. It's not a failed attempt when it happens; God wants us to be real with Him about the effect He's had in our lives.

Don't just gather information about people who have failed big or are in need—go be with them.

We'll see
what we spend the most time
looking for.

When you are with someone in need,
don't just be in proximity—be present.
Catch them. Don't try to teach them.
There's a big difference.

For some people, it's easier to make plans
than to make time. If this is you,
here's how to fix it: Make love your plan.
There's less to write down that way.

We don't need to wait for just the right moment to show up for others. We just need to be there, grab a parachute, and, when it's time, jump out of our shoes after people the way Jesus jumped out of Heaven to be with us.

We usually don't need all the plans we make. Sure, plans can help from time to time, but planning to love people is different than just loving people.

May 22

It doesn't matter what our faith looks like;
it matters what it is.

August 9

Jesus often uses our blind spots
to reveal Himself to us.

People who are becoming love stop faking it about who they are and where they are in their lives and their faith.

Faith isn't knowing what we can't see;
it's landing the plane anyway
rather than just circling the field.

God feels very strongly about us keeping
it real and transparent and honest about
where we actually are rather than faking it
and pretending we're someone
we only hope to be someday.

We have some guaranteed green lights that are always on: our noble desires, God's clear instructions in the Bible to love everybody always, His love for us, and the gift of each other.

God can use us
wherever we are.

August 6

Go with what you've got.
If God wants you to stay put,
He'll let you know.

The Bible is full of stories of people
who messed up. It seems like failure in the
world was a requirement
for success with God.

God may not give us
all the green lights we want,
but I'm confident
He gives us all the green lights
He wants us to have at the time.

People who are becoming love keep it real about who they are right now while living in constant anticipation about who God's helping them become.

You don't need to take all the steps,
just the next one.

We should all have beautiful ambitions for our lives and who we might become, but we also need to be careful not to be fooled into believing we've already arrived at a place in our faith we've only been thinking about going to someday.

Sometimes it's a good thing to pause. One of the writers in the Bible said to his friends that just because the door was open didn't mean it was for him to walk through. The difference between a prudent pause and persistent paralysis is a distinction worth knowing.

Have you noticed when people take
photographs of each other, the person
taking the picture is usually smiling too?
Check it out for yourself. I think God
does the same thing when He sees us.

August 2

At some point, we need to stop waiting for permission and go live our lives. God isn't stingy with His love, and He doesn't delight in seeing us uncomfortable either. Perhaps we don't get all the answers and confirmations we ask for because God loves seeing us grow.

God isn't trying to bust us when we fail
or when we act like posers. He doesn't
hang photographs of our mess-ups on the
refrigerator. He isn't in the business of
punishing us with reminders;
instead, He pursues us with love.

Don't let wanting one more "sign"
keep you from fulfilling your purpose.
God isn't surprised we want more
confirmation. He just hopes
we won't get stuck waiting for it.

God doesn't grimace at our failures;
He delights in our attempts.

Each day I start with the things I'm certain about and try to land my weight on those things. It always starts with a loving, caring God who is tremendously interested in me and the world I live in. I'm picky about what else I add after that.

We might think we need other people's permission or love or approval before we can live our lives and pursue our beautiful ambitions. It's both good and bad. It's good if it causes us to want to pursue Jesus' love and approval more. But it's bad if we miss out on who God uniquely made us to be so we can be who someone else thinks we should be.

God is less concerned about the people who admit their doubts than the ones who pretend they're certain.

God has never looked in your mirror or mine and wished He saw someone else.

Sometimes when we ask God for an answer, He sends us a friend. Figure out whom He's already sent to you.

Every time we fake it and aren't authentic,
we make God's love for us look fake too.
He doesn't want us to just look different.
He wants us to become love.

Figure out the couple of things you're
sure about and put all your weight on
those things. I've put all of mine on Jesus
because I figured out He was a green light
I could trust.

June 4

God isn't shaking His head in disapproval
as we make our way toward Him.
He's got His arms outstretched,
welcoming us home to Him with love.

July 27

Here's the deal: All those deep urgings you feel to step toward the beautiful, courageous thing you're afraid to do— you probably won't always have the chance. Now is the time. Your life, your experiences, and your faith are your green lights. Make your move.

I bet if we could hear what God is thinking, we'd hear Him whispering, "You've got this.
Just keep moving toward Me."

I once heard a friend say all opportunities come with expiration dates. If you don't grasp the opportunity in front of you, it's likely going to go away at some point.

Do you want to do something amazing
for God? Trade the appearance
of being close to God for the power
of actually being close to God.

Don't wait to join a movement.
A movement is just a bunch of people
making moves. Be a movement.
Figure out what your next move is going
to be then make it. No one is remembered
for what they only planned to do.

Quit talking a big game and go live a big faith. One of Jesus' friends said if we want to get it right, we need to live a life worthy of the calling we've received.

What delights you?
What fires your imagination?
What fills you with a deep sense of
meaning and purpose?
What draws you closer to God?
What is going to last in your life and in the
lives of others? Do those things.

June 8

Our call is to love God and the people around us while we live into the most authentic version of ourselves.

God has made us good at some things
and horrible at other things. He brings
joyful, beautiful, fun people into our lives
and a few difficult ones too. Sometimes
He changes the trajectory of our plans
by taking away what we've comfortably
known and letting us fly through valleys
that are deeper and narrower than any
we've been through before.

We weren't just an idea God hoped would work out someday. We were one of His most creative expressions of love ever.

July 22

I don't think God uses card tricks to get our attention. Rather, He gives us hopes and dreams and desires; then He gives us tenacity and resilience and courage.

People who are becoming love shun all the attention because they don't need it anymore. They realize bright lights don't need spotlights. Instead, they see every act of selfless love as a declaration of their faith.

July 21

Some people look for shooting stars or ladybugs landing on their noses as answers from God. Sure, He could communicate to us this way. But honestly, while these kinds of things have happened to me, they've never really felt like answers; they just felt like reminders.

People who are becoming love
come to see love as its own reward
simply because it pleases God.

What if we found out
God's big plan for our lives
is that we wouldn't spend so much
of our time trying to figure out
a big plan for our lives?
Perhaps He just wants us to love Him
and love each other.

Instead of evaluating what others are doing, people who are becoming love see them as people who are on their own adventure with God. They don't stop caring; they're just so busy engaging in what God is doing in the world, it doesn't matter anymore.

God's plans aren't ruined
just because our plans need to change.

God wants our hearts,
not our help.

July 18

God doesn't allow difficulties and hardship and ambiguity to happen to mess with our heads; He uses these circumstances to shape our hearts. He knows they are what cause us to grow because we are reminded of our absolute dependence upon Him.

Instead of saying you're a missionary, why
not just go somewhere to learn about your
faith from the people you find there
and be as helpful as you can be?

July 17

Most of us want more green lights than we have. It's easy to forget that our faith, life, and experiences are all the green lights we need.

June 15

We don't need to call
everything we do "ministry" anymore.
Just call it Tuesday. That's what people
who are becoming love do.

If we let them,
the hard places we navigate help us steer
a more purposeful course forward.
This has been God's idea for us all along.

Jesus' message to the world is as simple
as it is challenging: It's not about us
anymore; it's about Him.

People who are becoming love understand
God guides us into uncomfortable places
because He knows most of us are too
afraid to seek them out ourselves.

People who are turning into love don't need all the spin, because they aren't looking for applause or validation from others any longer. They've experienced giving away God's love as its own reward.

When our faith gets tested,
we have the chance to grow.
Stated differently, if we want
our faith to get stronger,
we need to navigate some deep places.

People who are becoming love don't need
to shout that they're working for Jesus
after every loving thing they do.
They give their love away freely without
any thought about who gets credit for it.

July 13

Every day we get to decide if we'll take it easy and fly over the mountaintops in our relationships or make ourselves better and find our way through the valleys.

Jesus doesn't need credit, and we shouldn't either. When the heavens themselves declare His glory, He doesn't need our endorsement.

I'm not saying everything needs to be risky in our lives, but we'd be well served if a few more things were riskier in our faith. Loving people we don't understand or agree with is just the kind of beautiful, counterintuitive, risky stuff people who are becoming love do.

No one keeps track of how many times they talk about sports and cars and music and food. We talk about what we love the most. People who are becoming love talk a lot more about what God's doing than what they're doing because they've stopped keeping score.

Playing it safe doesn't move us forward
or help us grow; it just finds us where we
are and leaves us in the same condition
it found us in. God wants something
different for us. His goal is never
that we'll come back the same. He's hoping
we'll return more dependent on Him.

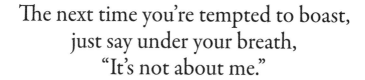

The next time you're tempted to boast,
just say under your breath,
"It's not about me."

Playing it safe and waiting for assurances
in our lives isn't necessarily bad;
it just isn't faith anymore.

"It's not about me."
Say it a dozen times a day.
Say it a thousand times a month.
Say it when you wake up and when you go
to sleep. Say it again and again:
"It's not about me.
It's not about me."

A lot of people think playing it safe
and waiting for all the answers before
they move forward is the opposite of
dangerous. I disagree. If our life and our
identity are found in Jesus, I think we can
redefine safe as staying close to Him.

"It's not about me." Say it when you bless a
meal or do something wonderful or selfless
or when you help hurting people.
Make it your anthem and your prayer.

July 8

Jesus never asked anyone to play it safe.
We were born to be brave.

We can either keep track of all the good
we've done or all the good God's done.
Only one will really matter to us.

The next time someone near you messes
up, pull them aside in private.
Don't give them a pile of instructions like
it's sheet music. Just give them
a hug. You'll be making grace and love
and acceptance finger memory
for them too.

People who turn into love don't keep
track. They don't memorize the good
or bad they or anyone else have done.
They memorize grace instead.

God makes people
and people make issues,
but people aren't issues.
They're not projects either.
People are people.

The promise of love and grace in our lives
is this: Our worst day isn't bad enough,
and our best day isn't good enough.
We're invited because we're loved,
not because we earned it.

Memorize grace.
Make it your muscle memory.

June 27

Everyone hits a couple of wrong notes;
keep playing your song.

July 4

Should we have a firm grip on doctrine
and know what the Bible speaks to
the world? You bet. Keep this in mind
though: Loving people the way Jesus did
is always great theology.

Stages, audiences, and platforms change us. People who are becoming love don't need any of it. It's not inherently bad to have all the stages, but we can end up playing to the wrong audience.

Mary ran to the tomb a couple of days after Jesus had been buried and rose again, and she thought Jesus was the gardener. He didn't embarrass her in front of everybody and tell her all the reasons why she was wrong. He didn't have a Bible study with her about it either. He just said her name: "Mary."

The early church made their own economy
by making themselves and their resources
available to everyone. They did this
because they were becoming love.

There is a quiet confidence in knowing we all hit a couple of wrong notes here and there. The report card on our faith is how we treat one another when we do.

Whether we want to or not, we end up memorizing what we do repeatedly. It's the way we were wired from the factory. Because this is how we're made, it's a great idea to pick actions worth repeating.

July 1

People who are becoming love fill their
lives with songs, practices, and habits that
communicate love, acceptance, grace,
generosity, whimsy, and forgiveness.
They repeat these actions
so often they don't even realize
they're doing it anymore.